A CONSTITUTIONAL TREATY FOR THE EU

The British Approach to the European Union Intergovernmental Conference 2003

Presented to Parliament by the
Secretary of State for Foreign and Commonwealth Affairs
By Command of Her Majesty
September 2003

Cm5934

£14.00

Foreword

This is a time of real significance for the European Union and for Britain.

In May next year, 10 new Member States will join the European Union, bringing an end to the Cold War division of the continent and creating an enlarged single market of over 450 million people.

For Britain, this means renewing partnerships with old friends, and forging new relationships with others. For the European Union, it will arguably be the most significant development since the foundation of the EEC.

Britain has been a champion of EU enlargement for many years. We wholeheartedly welcome it. But modernisation of Europe's decision-making structures is essential to make it a success.

That is why, in advance of this historic enlargement, all 25 Member States, new and old, will meet in an Intergovernmental Conference (IGC) to negotiate and to agree a Constitutional Treaty for the European Union. They will build on the text of the Convention on the Future of Europe (chaired by President Valéry Giscard d'Estaing), which Governments have said will be the starting point for negotiations. This in turn is based largely on the existing European Treaties, but with some important modifications.

Let me be clear: the Convention's end product – a draft Constitutional Treaty for the European Union – is good news for Britain. The Convention text spells out that the EU is a Union of nation States and that it only has those powers which Governments have chosen to confer upon it. It is not and will not be a federal superstate. The text reinforces the role of national Parliaments in the Union. And it proposes a new position of full-time President of the European Council, which will mean greater accountability to national governments as well as greater efficiency.

But the text is not perfect. Like many other Member States, there are some points in the Convention text which we will want to examine in more detail. And we could only accept a final text that made it clear that issues like tax, defence and foreign policy remain the province of the nation State. Provided there is clarity on these points, the reforms proposed by the Convention should be welcomed. They do not alter the fundamental constitutional relationship between the Member States and the Union, but they do promise that tomorrow's EU will not only be bigger, but should be also more effective.

Britain has a leading role in the European Union. We are stronger, richer and more secure in Europe. It is emphatically in our national interest that Britain continues to shape the key debates, as a new Europe is born.

We want a Europe that is outward looking, working in partnership and friendship with the United States and other allies. We want a Europe that continues to progress economically, delivering jobs and prosperity. We want a Europe that effectively tackles problems that do not recognise borders, such as people-trafficking, protecting the environment and organised crime. And for this we need a Europe with strong intergovernmental *and* supranational institutions to ensure that Europe continues to move in the right direction.

This approach is the foundation of the Government's approach to the 2003 Intergovernmental Conference, as set out in this White Paper. I look forward to discussing these issues with our European partners. I am confident that we will negotiate a new Constitutional Treaty that will promote the national, and the patriotic, interest. Like next year's enlargement of the Union, that will be good for Britain, and good for Europe.

Tony Blair
September 2003

Contents

Preface

On 4 October 2003, the Member States of the European Union will launch an Intergovernmental Conference (IGC) to draw up a new Treaty for the EU. EU leaders agreed in June that the draft Constitutional Treaty drawn up by the Convention on the Future of Europe was a good basis for starting in the IGC.[1]

The IGC will therefore take the final decisions on reform of the European Union, to make its institutions more transparent; more accountable; and more effective and efficient, and thus better able to meet the challenges of the 21st century.

This White Paper sets out how we have reached this point; what we expect the IGC to involve; and how Her Majesty's Government will approach the negotiations.

This White Paper includes explanations of EU terms, a passage on the structure and recent history of the EU, and a comprehensive glossary. And we have produced an accompanying leaflet providing a short summary of the main IGC issues and background. The full text of the Paper can also be accessed on the Foreign and Commonwealth Office website at **www.fco.gov.uk**.

Jack Straw
September 2003

---

[1] Thessaloniki European Council Conclusions, 19-20 June 2003, paragraph 5.

I. Britain in Europe

Benefits of the European Union

1. Our membership of the European Union is essential to our prosperity. It makes us part of one of the largest single markets in the world – a market which will grow further after the next round of enlargement, which will bring the EU to 25 Member States with 450 million people. That is a larger market than the United States and Japan combined. Our prosperity, and more particularly over 3 million jobs in the UK, depends on this market.[2] And the EU represents a huge proportion of the UK's trade: since we joined the EU in 1973, its share of our total trade has grown from 40 to 55%; we now export three times as much to the EU as to the US, and more to France and Germany than to the whole of the developing world.[3]

2. But the European Union is about much more than trade. Alongside NATO it has helped cement peace and stability across Europe after centuries of instability and conflict. It represents a model of democracy, tolerance and freedom for both the immediate neighbourhood and the wider world. It has played a critical role in the benign process of reform in the former Soviet bloc countries; helped many of those countries to real statehood for the first time in living memory; and has shown that sovereignty of nation states shared is sovereignty strengthened.

3. As the EU has grown beyond its role as a trading community, the Member States have realised collectively that there are many challenges that they can better tackle working together than separately.

4. Europe-wide problems like pollution or illegal immigration need Europe-wide solutions. We are now seeing the benefits of cooperating with our EU partners on a wide range of issues, from combating terrorism to ensuring the best deal for consumers. This joint work is there to make life safer and more secure for Europe's citizens. For example, action taken after 11 September 2001 to track down and prevent terrorist funding means our streets, airports and airlines are that much more secure. Similarly the rules underlying the single market mean that British citizens have similar rights whether they make a purchase in Leeds, Lyon or Lisbon. And if they do not in practice, we can enforce them in court.

5. The UK has global interests, and a significant role on the world stage. We are the world's fifth largest trading nation, with a permanent seat on the UN Security Council and membership of the G8. We can act alone or with non-EU partners. But on many foreign policy tasks – for example, encouraging the establishment of stable, open, democratic governments and institutions in the Western Balkans – we can best achieve our objectives by working with and through the EU. This is why we and our EU partners negotiate as a bloc in international trade

---

[2] Source: *UK jobs dependent on the EU*, Ardy, Begg and Hodson, European Institute, South Bank University, April 2000.
[3] In 2001 UK exports to the EU stood at $146 billion, and exports to the US at $43 billion. UK exports to France and Germany stood at $57 billion and to the developing world at $50 billion. Source: IMF.

or environmental negotiations, and why we have been leading the way, with France, in developing the EU's defence capabilities.

Benefits of engagement

6. Her Majesty's Government has a positive vision of Europe: of nation states, proud of their heritage and their individuality, pooling their sovereignty for the peace and prosperity of the continent. This vision is widely shared, not least by the ten states that will join the Union in May next year. Most of these countries have only recently emerged from the shadow of Soviet tyranny. They are fiercely protective of their independence. But they see the benefits of working with their neighbours through the EU, not least as enhancing that independence.

7. By positive engagement with our European partners, the Government is able to make that vision a reality. Through alliances with others, and through negotiation and compromise, we are winning the arguments on the policy issues which matter. We were the strongest supporters of enlargement, and secured it in Copenhagen last December, on the timetable we had proposed. We launched the Lisbon Economic Reform Agenda, which has brought about important new areas of market liberalisation. And in June, we secured one of the most important reforms of the Common Agricultural Policy in the history of the EU.

8. We should be under no illusions: withdrawing from the EU would be a disaster for this country. It would damage our prosperity. We would lose jobs and lose influence. It wouldn't just mean less trade with the EU, but globally: for the English speaking world, the UK is a gateway to Europe and its single market. If that gate were closed, much of their business would go elsewhere. Outside the EU, we would have less, not more, control of our economy – because to continue to trade with the Union, we would still have to be bound by its rules. But we would end up with much less say in shaping them.

9. The EU underpins the security and future prosperity of this country. It is at the heart of our efforts to open markets, combat crime and tackle pollution. And the Government believes that the UK should be at the heart of the EU, shaping the agenda and advancing our objectives.

What has the EU done for us?

Wealth: The EU now gives the UK access to a vast single market of some 370 million people across Europe. It will be bigger still when the current applicants join – 450 million people from 2004 – more than the US and Japan combined. We export three times as much to the EU as to the US, and more to France and Germany than to the whole of the developing world.

Jobs: More than *three million jobs* in UK companies are estimated to depend on the EU. Each previous enlargement of the EU has resulted in greater prosperity – research estimates that the next enlargement should create 300 000 new jobs in the current EU countries.[4] Two million people in Britain are employed by foreign investors – many attracted to the UK by our EU membership.

Peace and stability: The EU, along with other international organisations like NATO and the United Nations, has helped to make a repeat of the First and Second World Wars unthinkable. As the Union enlarges, it *reinforces peace, democracy and freedom* across Europe. When the UK joined the European Community in 1973, Spain, Portugal and Greece were ruled by dictatorships, and most of the ten countries about to join the EU were Soviet satellites. All of these countries are now free, democratic partners.

Security: 30 years ago law enforcement cooperation with the rest of Europe was slow and ineffective. Escaping abroad often meant escaping justice. Europol (an EU criminal intelligence organisation) and Eurojust (an EU body for co-ordinating investigations and prosecutions) have already led to the arrest of drug traffickers, child pornographers and suspected Al Qa'ida terrorists. Fugitives from British justice will soon be brought back quickly to the UK as a result of the European arrest warrant.

---

[4] Source: *Profiting from EU enlargement: the costs and benefits in perspective*, Heather Grabbe, Centre for European Reform for the European Round Table of Industrialists, July 2001.

Freedom to work and travel across Europe: In 1973, 'the Continent' appeared to many a distant and rather inaccessible place. You often needed a visa to travel there. British people now have the right to travel, work, study and live visa-free throughout the EU. UK residents will make around *forty million trips* to other EU countries this year. 100 000 Britons are currently working in other EU Member States. 234 000 UK pensioners draw their pensions in other EU countries. On average, 10 000 UK students study abroad in the EU each year. And, contrary to fears expressed at each previous enlargement, many more Britons have gone to live elsewhere in the EU than EU nationals have to the UK.

Consumer benefits: The EU has also introduced rules to protect consumers. British *citizens have guaranteed rights* whenever they buy anything throughout the European Union. Many prices have been driven down too thanks to the EU. The cost of making a call or taking a flight across Europe has been cut in recent years because of EU rules encouraging liberalisation and greater competition. And the single market has helped bring us greater choice in our shops.

A better deal on holidays: Today, Britons travelling to the continent enjoy benefits that were unheard of when the UK joined the EU in 1973. British travellers are now covered for *emergency hospital treatment* on holiday in the EU by the E111 scheme. The blue EU channel allows travellers to move more quickly through customs. Package tour operators also have to meet certain advertising criteria thanks to EU rules – if they change your holiday, or cancel it, they must provide compensation.

A cleaner environment: Pollution respects no national borders. Cooperation with EU partners is *helping to tackle cross-border pollution* and other threats to our environment. In 1973, sulphur dioxide emissions (one of the key pollutants forming acid rain) were measured in the UK at 6.1 million tonnes. By 1999, these had fallen to 1.2 million tonnes. And since the UK joined the EU there has been concerted action to clean up beaches, rivers and drinking water.

30 years of Membership

Over our thirty years of membership, the objective of working together to tackle cross-Europe issues has been pursued by two main bodies: the **Council of Ministers**, the principal decision making body, consisting of representatives of the Member States; and the **European Commission**, which has responsibility for making proposals to the Council and implementing the Council's decisions. The other important parts of the EU's structure are a Court of Justice to resolve disputes and an Assembly of national Parliamentarians – now the European Parliament.

The Treaty of Rome conferred certain *competences,* or powers, on these institutions. In effect, the Member States collectively decided to give these institutions certain supranational powers to take decisions in particular areas. Community Law – what is now EU Law – is based on the Treaties, the decisions made by the institutions, and the case law of the European Courts since 1957. It has *primacy* over national law to the extent of any inconsistency. This is consistent with the principle of international law whereby a State may not plead its national law obligations to escape its international law obligations, and prevents countries from going back on commitments they have made to each other. This primacy of EC law was a key condition for our membership – as it is for all Member States; and is enshrined in UK law by Section 2 of the European Communities Act 1972.

The overall result is a structure which uses supranational rules and institutions to create a delicate system of checks and balances. It protects the vital national interests of its members by giving each of them a veto over treaty change, but also allows them to remove their veto in certain areas in the interests of progress, and to rely on bodies required by the Treaties to be impartial and independent (the Commission and the European Court of Justice) to enforce the rules in the interests of all.

The basic framework has changed very little over this thirty-year period. The democratic accountability of the EU has been strengthened through the transformation of the Assembly into a fully-fledged, directly-elected **European Parliament**. And the role of the Member States in setting the strategic agenda of the Union has been strengthened through their regular meetings at the level of Heads of State or Government in the form of the **European Council**.

The most significant change to the EU in the last thirty years is enlargement. We joined with Ireland and Denmark in 1973 to turn a Community of six into one of nine. The addition of Greece, Portugal and Spain in the 1980s brought that to 12. The accession of Austria, Finland and Sweden in 1995 makes today's 15. But from 1 May next year, the EU will have grown to include 25 Member States. And still more countries, including Romania, Bulgaria and Turkey, are waiting to join this unique, European, success story.

Changes to the Treaties

The Member States have agreed successive Treaties to extend the benefits of cooperation to other areas.

The *Single European Act* of 1986 set out to complete the Single Market and initiated cooperation in environment policy and foreign policy. It also strengthened the role of the European Parliament, introducing a "cooperation procedure" in ten policy areas and requiring the European Parliament's approval for the accession of new EU Member States, as well as for the conclusion of association agreements with countries outside the EU. The Act extended QMV to 12 new or existing articles.

The *Treaty of Maastricht* of 1992 established the Common Foreign and Security Policy and cooperation in Justice and Home Affairs and paved the way for the single currency. It also formally renamed the European Community as the European Union. Maastricht extended the Union's competence to a number of new policy areas, including economic and monetary policy, social policy, education, vocational training and youth, culture, public health, consumer protection, Trans-European Networks, industry and development. Maastricht introduced the co-decision procedure for the European Parliament, and extended or introduced QMV to 30 policy areas.

The *Treaty of Amsterdam* of 1997 added provisions on social policy and employment and moved asylum and immigration to the first pillar. It incorporated the Schengen agreement and endorsed "the progressive framing of a common defence policy". It also provided for closer cooperation between sub-groups of Member States, though not in foreign policy. Amsterdam abolished the cooperation procedure, and instead simplified and extended the co-decision procedure. It extended QMV to 16 new and existing policy areas.

The *Treaty of Nice* of 2001 adjusted the institutions in the light of the EU's enlargement. It reweighted the system of Council voting and the number of seats in the European Parliament, as well as streamlining the structure and functioning of the European Commission. Nice developed the provisions for enhanced cooperation and extended QMV to a further 31 areas.

II. What is changing in Europe?

Why more treaty change?

10. The EU works. But it could work better. It has been a success – in helping to stabilise a continent that had been wracked by war and creating the conditions for economic growth. But that very success has given rise to new challenges.

11. As the governments of Europe have chosen to cooperate through the EU in more areas, they have agreed new treaties, adding new layers of legal complexity. So the EU Treaties must be made more coherent and easier to understand. The EU's success has also attracted new members, putting further strain on the Union's institutions. So those institutions must be reformed to be efficient and effective in an EU of 25 or more.

a. Developing needs of Europe's citizens

12. The Europe of 50 years ago had been shattered by war. Its people sought stability, to rebuild their houses, farms and factories. The European Coal and Steel Community – the precursor of the EU – was designed to put the war-fighting materials of former enemies under joint control and bind them in mutual prosperity. The benefits of this model were extended by the EEC to agriculture and other sectors. In 1992, this became a genuine single market for goods, services, capital and people.

13. The success of this cooperation in the economic sphere has led the Member States of the EU to work together in other spheres. This joint work – such as in foreign policy or in the fight against crime – has complemented, not replaced, the work of national governments. But it has required new EU Treaties, adding to the original.

14. This has led to two challenges. First, the EU's framework has become too complex and unwieldy. Second, now the EU has come to play a more important role in people's lives, they expect more clarity on its workings.

15. There is no single document to which someone could turn to find out about the Union's aims and objectives or processes of decision making.

16. The EU needs a clearer statement of what it does, why it does it and how. Its legal structure should be made easier to understand. And Europe's citizens and businesses should know what powers national governments have conferred on the EU, and what powers they have kept for themselves.

17. On the second challenge: the EU now plays a greater role in people's lives. They therefore expect it to be more responsive to their needs and to listen to their concerns. So the Union must become more open and better understood. This is the test of the EU's legitimacy.

18. Twenty-four years ago the European Parliament had its first direct elections. Europe's citizens expect to see the role of that Parliament improved, in representing their views and holding the other institutions to account. National Parliaments should also play a crucial role in connecting people to the EU. Their role in the EU's decision making process should be strengthened.

b. Challenges of Enlargement

"This is an extraordinary moment in Europe's history... When we look back at the history of Europe over many hundreds of years, and in particular the history of the 20th century, and we reflect on the war, and devastation, and disaster, and conflict, and then we realise that today we are reuniting Europe, I think it is truly a moment that we can be very proud of and offers us huge hope for the future."

Prime Minister Tony Blair, Copenhagen, December 2002

19. On 1 May 2004, Cyprus, Czech Republic, Estonia, Hungary, Latvia, Lithuania, Malta, Poland, Slovakia and Slovenia will all join the EU. When they do so, they will bring to an end the decades of division that was the Cold War and most of Europe will be reunited. Romania and Bulgaria expect to join the EU in 2007. Turkey is a candidate. Others will follow.

20. The UK has always been a strong supporter of enlargement. We have played a leading role in moving the process forward. The enlargement negotiations began under the UK's Presidency of the EU in 1998. The Government then played a crucial role in bringing them to a successful conclusion in Copenhagen in December last year.

21. In a speech in Warsaw in October 2000, Prime Minister Tony Blair was the first EU leader to call for the new Member States to join in time to participate in the 2004 European Parliament elections. This ambitious vision is now becoming a reality.

22. Enlargement will bring many benefits to this country and to Europe as a whole. An enlarged EU will boost European stability, security, trade and jobs. Independent research estimates that enlargement could add £1.75bn to UK GDP and create over 300,000 jobs across the fifteen current Member States.[5]

23. But enlargement also brings challenges. The EU's institutions were built for a Union of just six members. Some of those institutions are creaking in a Union of 15. In a Union of 25 – or more – they will be under even greater pressure.

---

[5] Sources: *Profiting from EU enlargement: the costs and benefits in perspective*, Heather Grabbe, Centre for European Reform for the European Round Table of Industrialists, July 2001.

24. The system of rotating the Council Presidency between the Member States every six months is a good example. Supporters argue that holding the Presidency brings the EU to life for the citizens of that country. This might have made sense when countries held the Presidency every three years. It makes less sense in a Union of 25, when a Member State will hold the Presidency every twelve and a half years, just once or twice in a generation. We need a new system that can bring coherence and consistency to the Union's work.

c. The UK's views

25. The Government recognises the need to reform the EU. We want to make the EU more effective because we recognise that it is essential to the future well-being of British citizens. And we recognise that to be more effective, the EU must adapt to new challenges; to the greater demands made of it by its citizens; and to its enlarged membership.

"the objective for Britain... is a Europe that is strong, effective and democratic. This requires a strengthening of Europe at every level: Council, Commission, Parliament and Court. And the test we should apply to each issue is not whether it tilts the balance towards national Governments or European government. But rather in each case: does it strengthen Europe; does it make it more effective; does it make it more democratic?"

Prime Minister Tony Blair, Cardiff, November 2002

d. But what if there is no change?

26. If a new Treaty cannot be agreed, or ratified, then the EU would still carry on under its current arrangements; and it would have the same functions as it has today. It would not collapse. But the failure to reform would undermine the existing institutional balance of the EU. In particular, with 10 more countries joining the EU and more expected in the future, the Council – the body representing national governments – would become far more unwieldy.

27. If the Member States did not agree a new Treaty, they would have missed a great opportunity to make the EU more efficient, simpler to understand, more accountable to the European and national Parliaments, and better prepared to function effectively with 25 and more members.

Why enlarge the EU?

It will make the UK, the EU and the new members wealthier.
Research estimates that UK GDP could increase by up to £1.75 billion.
In the new Member States, economic integration will raise output and growth
rates by stimulating entrepreneurship, investment and technology transfers.
This could add between £16 billion and £35 billion to their GDP.[6]

It will bring new trade and investment opportunities for the UK.
Since 1990, UK trade with the accession countries has increased nearly
10 times as fast as with the rest of the world.

It is transforming Europe, for the better. Stability and prosperity are
growing beyond the current borders of the EU, as many countries work
to meet the criteria for membership.

It is transforming future EU members for the better. In 1989, travel
was a privilege in Poland, consumer goods in short supply, inflation at
600%. Now twice the number of Poles go to university, they travel widely
and inflation is about 1%. All this in 13 years, underpinned by the process
of joining the EU. Similarly, economic output in the Baltics is growing
quickly. Yet for other countries bordering Russia, once all part of the
USSR, output is lower than the 1990 level and GDP is at one quarter of
the levels of the Baltic states.

**It shows that the founding principles of the EU – peace, stability and
security – remain valid.** It costs us far less financially, politically and
socially, to support our neighbours' transition to stable democracies and
open economies, than it does to rebuild them after conflict.

It will mean a cleaner Europe. Water and air quality will improve as
new Member States have to meet EU standards. Good news for the
millions of British holiday makers who will travel to the new members.

It will mean a level playing field for British business as businesses in
the new members become subject to the same EU standards on health
and safety, the environment, consumer protection and state aids.

---

[6] Sources: *Profiting from EU enlargement: the costs and benefits in perspective*, Heather Grabbe, Centre for European
Reform for the European Round Table of Industrialists, July 2001.

It will bring new partners in the fight against people trafficking and drugs as new members have to meet EU standards on border controls and cooperation against serious crime and terrorism. They are invaluable partners. For example in June 2003 Czech police arrested 15 facilitators and 130 illegal immigrants, the culmination of an investigation into a gang believed to have smuggled at least 400 immigrants into Western Europe. This success was achieved by European cooperation.

It helps improve human rights. New EU members had to meet the EU criteria on human rights before they were allowed to even start negotiating to join the EU. All 10 accession countries joining the EU next year have signed and ratified the European Convention on Human Rights and Protocol 13 to the European Convention on Human Rights, which outlaws the death penalty in all circumstances.

The EU as a Treaty-based organisation

The EU is a Treaty-based organisation. This means that all EU actions are based on Treaties which have to be unanimously agreed between Member States. The EU cannot take any action unless Member States, and their national parliaments, have approved the specific Treaty base which allows it to do so.

Since the EU Treaties are agreed by unanimity, any changes to them must be decided in the same way. The mechanism for changing EU Treaties is an Intergovernmental Conference (IGC). Representatives of all Heads of Government meet to discuss and negotiate amendments to the Treaties. This takes place over a period of several months, or even years. Only when all Member States agree is the new Treaty ready to be signed.

Once signed, the Treaty must then be ratified according to the distinct constitutional arrangements of each of the Member States. In the UK, amendments to the EU Treaties must undergo a rigorous process of Parliamentary scrutiny before they can be ratified.

When the amendments have been approved and ratified by all Member States, the new provisions can enter into force.

III.
History and future process

Nice

28. The last Intergovernmental Conference was concluded in Nice, in 2000, to make some institutional preparations for enlargement. It put into place reforms to the voting arrangements in the Council of Ministers and the extension of qualified majority voting (QMV) to some new policy areas.

29. Nice explicitly recognised that future changes to the EU's structure could be necessary to make enlargement a success. In December 2000, EU leaders adopted a declaration calling for a deeper and wider debate about the future of the European Union, followed by an Intergovernmental Conference in 2004.

Laeken

30. In December 2001, the Laeken European Council followed the Nice declaration with a more detailed statement on the Future of Europe. This recognised the need to reform the EU's institutional structure in the run-up to enlargement, and to reconnect the EU with its citizens. To take forward the debate on the Future of Europe as broadly and openly as possible in the run-up to the Intergovernmental Conference, the Laeken Declaration called for a Convention to be established in order better to prepare the ground for Member States. Laeken identified four particular areas for the Convention to examine:

- a better, clearer definition of the EU's competences;
- simplification of its legal instruments;
- greater democracy, transparency and efficiency;
- the possible need for a Constitution for the EU.

The Treaty of Nice

The Treaty of Nice, signed in 2001, made various changes to the EU's institutions in order to pave the way for enlargement. These included:

- A **reweighting of votes** in the Council of Ministers to include the new Member States. This was supplemented by a population safeguard (so a decision is only passed if supported by a majority of Member States representing at least 62% of the total population of the EU).

- Agreement to streamline the **size of the Commission**. To avoid it becoming too unwieldy, the next College of Commissioners will contain only one Commissioner per Member State. When the EU reaches 27 members, the number of Commissioners will be less than the total number of Member States.

- Agreement on a new **distribution of seats in the European Parliament**, to take effect for the 2004-9 EP Term. The ceiling on seats was extended to 732 to accommodate the new Member States.

- **Qualified Majority Voting** in the Council of Ministers and **co-decision** by the European Parliament were extended to ensure that decision making in an enlarged EU continues to be efficient and accountable.

The Convention

31. The Convention started its work in February 2002. The British Government and representatives of the British Parliament all played a very active role. After a year and a half of long and vigorous debates, the Convention was judged to have fulfilled its mandate by the Thessaloniki European Council of 20 June 2003. It produced a draft Constitutional Treaty for the EU. This revised, brought together and rearranged the existing EU Treaties into a single text, split into four parts. Valéry Giscard d'Estaing presented the final versions of Parts I and II to EU leaders at Thessaloniki. And after some further technical work, final versions of Parts III and IV were presented to the Italian Presidency on 18 July. These have been presented to Parliament in Command papers: No 5872 on 7 July, containing Parts I and II, and No 5897 on 12 August containing all Parts.

Convention composition and process

The membership of the Convention reflected its aims to promote a wide-ranging debate about the future direction of the EU. This was the first time that representatives from a broad spectrum of countries and political groups had come together to discuss Treaty change in an open, public forum.

The existing Member States, the accession countries joining the EU in 2004, and the candidate countries, Bulgaria, Romania and Turkey, all contributed actively to the Convention's successful outcome.

Each of the 28 countries fielded delegates from their Governments and national Parliaments, as well as opposition parties and second Parliamentary chambers. The Convention included representatives from the European Parliament, the Commission, the Economic and Social Committee and the Committee of the Regions. In all, 105 members, plus alternates, met to debate the EU's future.

The UK Government representative was the Leader of the House, and former Minister for Europe, the **Rt Hon Peter Hain MP**. His alternate was **Baroness Scotland of Asthal**, Minister of State in the Home Office.

Like other national Parliaments, Westminster had two representatives: **Gisela Stuart MP** (Labour) and **Rt Hon David Heathcoat-Amory MP** (Conservative).

Their alternates were: **Lord Tomlinson** (Labour) and **Rt Hon Lord Maclennan of Rogart** (Liberal Democrat).

The Convention's work was divided into three phases. In early 2002, it began with a "listening" phase. This involved a programme of wide consultation with individuals and organisations representing civil society across Europe. Toward the end of 2002 this was followed by an "analytical phase". The Convention split into working groups to consider in detail the most important issues, such as defence, economic governance and subsidiarity.

At the beginning of 2003 the Convention moved into its final "drafting phase". Its conclusions, shaped by the work of the earlier phases, took the form of a draft Treaty. First drafts were drawn up by the Convention's Praesidium, a steering group consisting of the Convention's President, Valéry Giscard d'Estaing; the two Vice Presidents, Jean-Luc Dehaene and Giuliano Amato; plus representatives of the Convention's component groups (members of national parliaments, the European Parliament, the European Commission, and national governments). The Labour MP Gisela Stuart represented national parliamentarians from all participating countries on the Praesidium together with John Bruton of Ireland.

At each stage, the Convention's members had the opportunity to comment on the drafts with written suggestions or in debate during Plenary sessions. In keeping with the Convention's spirit of openness and transparency, all the Praesidium's drafts, and members' comments, were published on the Convention website.

Parliament and international treaties

All Treaties, including EU Treaties, are laid before Parliament, which has the right to examine and debate them in detail. All previous EU Treaties have been the subject of extensive examination and debate by Parliament.

A Treaty can only have force in UK law through an Act of Parliament. So Parliament must be satisfied that a Treaty is in the national interest before that Treaty can be implemented in national law. Without the consent of Parliament, no new legislation can be enacted. This means that MPs will be able to examine line by line what is in the final Treaty; and only with their assent will effect be given to the new Treaty in terms of transposition into UK law.

The ultimate guarantee of Parliamentary sovereignty lies in the power of Parliament to repeal all or any of the Acts which give effect to the EU Treaties in this country.

Under the UK's constitutional arrangements, Parliament makes the law. In certain circumstances Parliament has decided that particular laws should come into operation only after a referendum has been held. In practice, these have been held where there is a wholly new constitutional structure proposed – but not otherwise. So referendums have been held in Scotland, Wales and Northern Ireland so that people there could decide whether they wanted a Parliament or Assembly for their country; regional and local referendums can – and have – been held so that people can choose whether to have, for example, a Regional Assembly or Mayor, or stick with the current arrangements. Consistent with this principle, only one UK-wide referendum has ever been held. This was in 1975, when the question was whether the UK should stay in or withdraw from the EU. (The result was a two to one majority in favour of staying in.) Similarly, the present government is committed to holding a referendum on the Euro.

However, referendums have never been held to approve changes to the existing institutions of which we are members. Thus, no referendum was held on any of the Single European Act, Maastricht, Amsterdam or Nice.

The Single European Act and Maastricht, in the Government's view, involved changes within the operation of the EU greater than any likely to flow from this IGC. So, in line with the approach of previous administrations, the Government does not believe that there is a case for a referendum on the draft Constitutional Treaty. The proposed changes, though important, do not involve any fundamental change in the relationship between the European Union and Member States.

The constitutional arrangements in other Member States are a matter for them. Some Member States hold referendums on EU treaty changes, some do not.

Convention: Europe and the Regions

As well as consulting with the representatives of local government, the Government worked closely with the devolved administrations in formulating its approach to the Convention. The Joint Ministerial Committee on Europe, chaired by the Foreign Secretary and on which Ministers from each of the devolved administrations sit, met on several occasions to consider issues arising out of the Convention. Recognising the role of the regions in strengthening the EU's democratic legitimacy, the Committee commissioned a paper on "Europe and the Regions" which was presented to Convention by Peter Hain in February. Amongst other proposals, this advocated more thorough consultation by the European Commission of regional and local authorities at the pre-legislative stage, as well as measures to enhance the effectiveness of the Committee of the Regions.

Future Process – the Intergovernmental Conference

32. The framework for the coming Intergovernmental Conference was decided by Member States at the Thessaloniki European Council. European Leaders agreed that the draft Constitutional Treaty drawn up by the Convention was "a good basis" for starting negotiations in the IGC. They mandated the Italian Presidency of the EU to start the IGC in October. The conclusions went on: "The Conference should complete its work and agree the Constitutional Treaty as soon as possible and in time for it to become known to European citizens before the June 2004 elections for the European Parliament."

33. The Member States also decided that the ten countries due to join the EU in May next year should participate fully in the IGC "on an equal footing with the current Member States". The Constitutional Treaty, which the IGC should agree, will be signed by the Member States of the enlarged Union as soon as possible after the ten new members join in May. The other three candidates for EU membership will participate in the IGC as observers.

34. The IGC will be conducted by the Heads of State or Government of the Member States, assisted by their Foreign Ministers. A representative of the European Commission will also participate in the meetings. The European Parliament will be closely associated and involved in the IGC's work.

35. As in all complex negotiations, each participant will have to make compromises in order to agree a package acceptable to all. Each participating Government will have its own objectives. There will be different perspectives and lively debate. But there is also a great deal on which the 25 Member States and Acceding States already agree. The Government believes that the auguries are good that the IGC will agree a new Treaty for a more efficient and accountable EU.

36. But the Government would not agree to a new Treaty which was not in the UK's interests. Nor could we be made to do so. Any new Treaty will have to be agreed by unanimity. So each country, including the UK, has a veto.

Parliament and the IGC

37. Parliament was involved in the Convention on a number of levels, from the national parliamentary representatives, who gave progress reports to a specially constituted Standing Committee on the Convention, to Ministers being held to account by the European Scrutiny and EU Select Committees. The Government responded to Committee Reports, and deposited for scrutiny the draft Treaty Articles. In addition, considerable parliamentary time was spent debating the Convention, on the floor of both Houses and in Westminster Hall in four separate debates.

38. It will be important that Parliament is involved as fully as possible during the preparations for the IGC, and as it proceeds. This White Paper is a significant first step. The Foreign Secretary has been working closely with the European Scrutiny Committee (House of Commons) and the European Union Committee (House of Lords), and separately with Graham Allen MP, on ways in which Parliament's role can be strengthened. He has, for example, welcomed the suggestion of Jimmy Hood MP, Chair of the European Scrutiny Committee, that a Standing Committee on the IGC be created, following the successful work of the Standing Committee on the Convention. He also agreed that there should be ample time for debate on the IGC, as there had been in the Convention.

39. The Government is supplementing this formal consultation process with an online public consultation exercise as it prepares for the IGC. An electronic forum[7] is providing an opportunity for the public, parliamentarians, academics and think tanks to feed in their thoughts. The Hansard Society is acting as an independent monitor to help ensure an open and transparent exercise.

40. As with all previous EU Treaties, Parliament will, of course, examine whatever Treaty is agreed at the IGC, and decide whatever legislation is required to give effect to it.

---

[7] The forum can be found at **www.europe.gov.uk**.

IV. The Convention Outcome and Detailed Issues for the IGC

a. The Convention outcome – overview

41. The Convention outcome was a good result for the UK, reflecting the active and constructive role we took. The Government will seek to build on this in the IGC.

42. The Convention's draft meets important British goals:

    - The draft Treaty consolidates the existing EU Treaties into a single logically ordered text, which sets out what the EU is, what its objectives are and how it will strive to achieve them. The text replaces the Maastricht Treaty's three "pillars" with a single Treaty structure. The draft Treaty streamlines the number of EU legal instruments.

    - The draft Treaty sets out a more transparent and accountable structure for the EU. It includes a definition of the Union's competences, which makes clear where the EU can and cannot act. It strengthens the role of national Parliaments through a new procedure to reinforce subsidiarity, that is, the principle whereby, in policy areas where competence is shared between the Union and Member States, the Union should act only when "the objectives of the intended action cannot be sufficiently achieved by the Member States" alone. National parliaments will have a mechanism to send back proposals for EU laws if they do not add value.

    - The draft Treaty makes it clear that the national governments of Member States remain in control. The Union's powers clearly derive from the Member States; and the draft Treaty preserves the principle that the most important decisions on EU issues are taken, by unanimity, by the Governments of Member States.

    - The draft Treaty provides for a more efficient EU. It creates a full-time Chair of the Council of Ministers, which will lead to greater continuity and coherence in the Union's actions, and ensure that the agenda decided upon by Member States is delivered. These improvements in decision-making will be essential to the success of the enlarged EU.

43. Like most other Member States, the UK does not support every proposal put forward in the Convention. Important issues still need to be determined, as European leaders made clear at Thessaloniki. Some of these are areas of unfinished business, where the Convention has not worked through the detail of its proposals. Some are ideas with which we disagree. And some are issues which require further technical, including important legal, work.

b. Main proposals to be considered by the IGC

i. Treaty structure

44. The 1992 Treaty on European Union (or 'Maastricht Treaty') created a structure for the EU based on three "pillars". The first pillar was the current European Communities (broadly economic areas such as the single market, trade, the environment, agriculture and competition rules); the second was the Common Foreign and Security Policy (CFSP); and the third was cooperation in the field of Justice and Home Affairs (JHA). This structure had the advantage of keeping the special, intergovernmental arrangements for CFSP and JHA distinct from the rest of the EU's activity.

45. First pillar matters are governed by the 1957 Treaty of Rome, amended by subsequent Treaties. Second and third pillar matters are currently governed by the 1992 Maastricht Treaty on European Union. Subsequent EU Treaties have amended this structure, shifting policies from one pillar to another. Increasingly, this system of two Treaties and three pillars has come to be seen as overly-complicated and unwieldy. As mentioned above, it means there is no single text to which citizens, businesses or civil society organisations can refer.

46. The Convention on the Future of Europe therefore proposed dismantling the three pillars and replacing them with a single Treaty and a unified structure. The Government supports the aim of simplifying the EU and believes that this proposal could help to achieve that aim. But this should not mean that all spheres of EU activity should be treated in the same way. We support a single Treaty structure, but only if this does not compromise special arrangements for CFSP and some parts of JHA.

ii. Legal personality

47. Currently, only two parts of the EU – the European Community and Euratom – have express extensive legal personality. This enables them to act at international level, including the capacity to make treaties. The EU as a whole has a degree of inferred legal personality and restricted power to make international agreements. (No international organisation has the same full legal personality enjoyed by nation states).

48. The Convention has proposed, as a consequence of its proposals for the EU to adopt a single, unified treaty structure, that the EU itself take on the degree of legal personality currently enjoyed by the European Community.

49. The Government recognises the advantages of clarity and simplicity that could come from conferring a single legal personality on the Union, both from the point of view of third countries, and from that of the EU's citizens. In particular, it should lead to simpler and quicker procedures for negotiating agreements through the EU. But any move to confer a single legal personality on the Union must be on the basis that distinct arrangements for Common Foreign and Security Policy, for certain

aspects of Justice and Home Affairs and for representation in international organisations are fully safeguarded. For example, the Government would not accept any proposal that meant giving up its permanent membership of the UN Security Council and the rights which go with that.

iii. Institutions

50. The Convention's institutional proposals are designed to provide a solid framework for the EU in the years to come. The most important institutional proposal in the Convention package, which the UK strongly supports, is for a full-time Chair of the European Council. This figure would take on the functions of the European Council presidency, which currently rotates around Member States every 6 months, and carry them out for a minimum period of $2^{1}/_{2}$ years. This will bring coherence and consistency to the EU's actions, and thereby give the Member States through the Council much greater capacity to give direction and momentum to the EU's agenda, for example on the Lisbon process.

51. The draft Treaty also provides for new arrangements for the presidency of the EU's sectoral Councils and for enacting legislation arising from their work. The IGC will need to work out the detail. The Government believes that these Councils should be chaired by representatives of Member States on the basis of equal rotation, coordinated by the full-time Council Chair. We also believe that these Councils should continue to legislate in their areas. Again, we believe that this would create greater coherence and consistency.

52. The Convention also proposes a new post of "Union Minister for Foreign Affairs", which would combine the roles of the current EU High Representative for the Common Foreign and Security Policy and the Commissioner for External Relations. The Government sees advantages in better coordination of external policy at EU level, but some outstanding points remain to be addressed: most importantly, how to ensure that the new post is properly accountable to Member States in the Council, and its relationship with the Commission. There is also an issue as to how exactly he is described.

53. The IGC will also discuss possible changes to the EU's budget. The Government will insist on preserving arrangements which ensure that revenues remain a matter for Member States and decisions on them subject to unanimity and national ratification. We will seek to ensure value for money for UK taxpayers by working to strengthen discipline and proper accountability in spending from the Budget.

iv. "Competences", "Subsidiarity" and the Role of National Parliaments

Competences

54. It is plainly important for the accountability and transparency of the Union that citizens should know clearly who does what and why. We

therefore welcome the proposals in the draft Treaty which make the division of powers (or "competences") between the EU's institutions and the Member States clearer than in previous Treaties.

55. The Convention's draft states in Article I-1 that the EU draws its powers from the Member States, rather than the other way round. And for the first time, there is an explicit statement (Article I-9) that powers not explicitly conferred upon the Union remain with the Member States. Also, for the first time, the text sets out a clear definition of the different types of competence: where the Member States have chosen to confer exclusive competence on the EU; where the Member States share competence with the EU; and where the EU can only take supporting action to help the Member States achieve their goals.

56. The draft for the most part clarifies rather than alters the current division of powers. But it also includes proposals to introduce some specific new competences, including for energy, intellectual property, sport and administrative cooperation. There is already some Union activity in these areas and creating specific provisions should lead to greater transparency and legal certainty. But we will need to consider, on a case by case basis, whether the conferral of specific powers on the EU is the best way to allow us to pursue Union objectives; and, if so, what the relevant new title should say.

Subsidiarity

57. The application of an important principle of competence – "subsidiarity" – is a priority for the Government. Subsidiarity is the principle whereby, in policy areas where competence is shared between Union and Member States, the Union should only act when "the objectives of the intended action cannot be sufficiently achieved by the Member States" alone. In other words, the Union should only get involved where it can add value.

58. European leaders first agreed to this principle of "subsidiarity" in the Treaty of Maastricht; it was strengthened at Amsterdam, and is emphatically restated in the Convention's draft Treaty, in Articles I-9 and III-160, and in a new Protocol on Subsidiarity and Proportionality. We welcome this.

59. The Convention agreed to go further: to introduce a mechanism to make sure the principle is enforced. This mechanism would allow national parliaments to examine proposals for EU legislation right at the start of the legislative process. If more than a third of them thought a proposal did not comply with the principle of subsidiarity, the Commission would be asked to review it. This is a very significant step. In practice it would be very difficult for the Commission to ignore the strongly-held views of one-third of the national Parliaments, or indeed for Governments to do so if the matter were to be discussed in the Council.

> *The House of Lords European Union Committee concluded in its twenty-first Report on 15 May that "it is clear that the balance of power in the European Union is going to shift from the Commission in favour of the Member States if the [Convention's] proposals... are adopted".[8]*

60. The Government was throughout the Convention a leading advocate both of ensuring subsidiarity is properly enforced and of strengthening the role of national parliaments in Europe. We also welcomed the recognition the Convention gave to the role of regional government and local government. We will continue to support these proposals in the IGC.

v. The Union's Policies

61. The IGC will consider proposals from the Convention in specific policy areas and the ways in which decisions are taken. These include: greater use of qualified majority voting; greater use of co-decision; the internal market; trade; economic governance; tax; social policy and social security; and justice and home affairs.

Greater Use of Qualified Majority Voting

62. An important proposal is for greater use of Qualified Majority Voting (QMV) for decision-making in the Council of Ministers. There is also a proposal for a clause which would allow the European Council to vote by unanimity to move any Treaty article to QMV. We oppose anything which would undermine the role of national parliaments in Treaty change.

63. The Government recognises, as it did, for example, at Nice, and as its predecessors did in the Single European Act and the Maastricht Treaty, that, as the Union grows in size, so decision-making by unanimity can become more difficult. QMV can help make it easier. Experience shows that QMV does not weaken Britain's position in Europe – we are rarely outvoted.

64. On the contrary, QMV has helped Britain pursue an agenda which is in our interests. The Single Market would never have been constructed without QMV, nor would many pieces of legislation have been passed on, for example, the environment or market liberalisation, or reform of the Common Agricultural Policy. In many areas, the use of majority voting has benefited the British economy.

65. We therefore welcome the use of QMV as the general rule for legislative proposals. It is clearly in Britain's interests for QMV to help us cooperate on issues such as asylum and illegal immigration, which require solutions at European level.

---

[8] Lords Select Committee on European Union, Twenty-First Report, "The Future of Europe: Constitutional Treaty – Draft Articles on the Institutions", HL 105, 15 May 2003, paragraph 11.

66. But we will insist that unanimity remain for Treaty change; and in other areas of vital national interest such as tax, social security, defence, key areas of criminal procedural law and the system of own resources (the EU's revenue-raising mechanism). Unanimity must remain the general rule for CFSP, as proposed in the final Convention text.

Greater Use of Co-decision

67. The IGC will also consider extending the right of co-decision by the European Parliament to all legislative proposals subject to QMV, including, for example, on structural funds, agriculture and fisheries. The European Parliament is directly elected by Europe's citizens; it is therefore right that it should have an appropriate role in the adoption of most European legislation. So we again agree that this is sensible as a general rule, but will want to look at the pros and cons of co-decision on a case by case basis.

68. Our approach to the extension of QMV and co-decision will therefore, as always, be to agree where it is in Britain's interests, but not to do so in areas where our vital national interests dictate otherwise.

What is QMV?

Qualified Majority Voting is a system of voting in the Council of Ministers. Under QMV, Member States are allocated a certain number of votes, depending on their size. Following the accession of the 10 new Member States next year, large countries like the UK will have 29 votes, whereas Malta (the smallest Member State) will have 3.

Out of a total of 345 votes, 258 votes will be required to pass legislation ("by a qualified majority"), or 88 to block legislation. For an act to be passed, over half of the Member States must vote in favour of the proposal, and they must represent at least 62% of the population of the Union.

There will be discussion at the IGC of alternatives to this three-pronged voting system agreed at Nice. The Convention proposed a "dual majority" voting system, under which Member States' voting weights would be based purely on population size. And, again, over half the Member States would need to support a proposal, representing 60% of the EU's population.

The Government remain content with the Nice system of voting. For all of its complications, it was the product of lengthy negotiations and agreed as part of a broader package. But we will consider any new proposal on its merits, looking for a balance between the ease with which legislation can be passed and blocked.

Internal Market

69. The current Treaties establish the central function of the European Community as the creation of a common (now referred to as internal) market and set the guiding principles which should be followed in establishing it. They also establish the key components of a common market and provide the framework under which action may be taken by the Community to further its establishment or take action to correct distortions within it.

70. With some exceptions, the internal market principles apply to all forms of commercial activity carried out within the boundaries of the Union, whether in the public or private sector. The Government believes that the actions taken by the Union to establish and develop the internal market have significantly benefited the UK, and contribute positively to economic reform in Europe.

71. The Government will aim to ensure that the four freedoms that underpin the internal market (free movement of goods, persons, services and capital) remain at the centre of all Union internal polices and their implementation. The number of exceptions to these internal market principles permitted in the new Treaty should be kept to a minimum.

Trade

72. The current Treaties provide the framework under which bilateral and international trade agreements are negotiated and concluded between the EU and third countries. They provide the legal base for the implementation of any necessary internal measures arising from such agreements and for certain other autonomous measures relating to international trade.

73. The Government is in favour of moves to reduce barriers in international trade. The new Treaty should establish clear parameters for Union action to promote trade and development and to remove trade barriers. But these parameters should not lead to an increase in the internal powers of the Union. Voting arrangements for the negotiation and conclusion of international agreements should mirror those required for the adoption of equivalent rules internally.

Economic Governance

74. Many of the issues discussed in the European Convention and raised in the draft Constitutional Treaty could have significant consequences for the future performance of EU economies. The draft Constitutional Treaty proposed by the Convention has proposed changes to the EU's existing system of economic governance and other aspects of the EU fiscal framework; the institutional balance between the Union and

Member States in economic policy coordination; and the role of the Eurogroup, the informal grouping of euro area finance ministers. The Government will oppose any such proposals which might lead to unnecessary rigidities or undermine the central role of Member States in determining their economic policies. It will work to ensure outcomes that will bolster stability, promote flexibility and enhance the ability of European countries to raise productivity and employment levels.

75. The draft Treaty does not alter the terms of the UK's Economic and Monetary Union protocol (allowing the UK to decide whether or not to join the euro). This will need formally to be re-adopted on the conclusion of the IGC.

Tax

76. The Government believes that the right of Member States to determine their own tax policies is a fundamental one. Tax matters are a key component of national sovereignty and vital to the social and economic wellbeing of the country. It is for this reason that the Government made a manifesto commitment to maintain the UK's tax veto. And that is why, in the IGC, the Government will insist that tax matters continue to be decided by unanimity.

Social Policy and Social Security

77. The current Treaties provide for legislation on the social security rights of workers who move within the Community, working conditions and employment relations and on combating various forms of discrimination. Most of the legislation under the relevant Articles can only be adopted by the unanimous agreement of the Member States.

78. There are significant differences between social systems in the EU, which reflect national traditions and choices. The existing voting arrangements in the social field respect this diversity while facilitating freedom of movement, equality of treatment and fair working conditions within the Union. It is the Government's view that they should be retained in the IGC.

Justice and Home Affairs

79. The Government has long advocated EU action against organised crime, terrorism and illegal immigration. The EU also needs to work together to create a more effective asylum system. Shared problems need shared solutions. With the right reforms in place, the EU's enlargement offers the opportunity to build a safer and more secure Europe.

80. The existing Treaties already provide for extensive cooperation at EU level. The Maastricht Treaty on European Union brought, for the first time, cooperation on justice and home affairs within the Union. The Treaty of Amsterdam extended cooperation on immigration and asylum issues and refined the framework for police and judicial cooperation.

81. The Convention's proposals would be another important step forward. A single, simplified Treaty structure would provide a coherent long-term framework for cooperation on justice and home affairs issues. The Government particularly welcomes the inclusion in the draft Treaty of the principle of mutual recognition of different legal systems as the cornerstone of police and judicial cooperation between Member States. We also welcome the focus on improving operational cooperation between Member States' law enforcement bodies, and on strengthening the role of national parliaments in the decision making process.

82. It is also important that, on asylum and immigration, the new Treaty establishes the framework for identifying quickly and fairly persons in genuine need of international protection while tackling abuses of the asylum system. QMV would be an important tool for speeding up decision making in this area.

83. The new Treaty would also provide for minimum standards at EU level to protect British citizens facing criminal proceedings in another Member State. The scope of the provision in the draft Treaty, however, is wider than this and it is subject to QMV. The Government will seek to define where the EU should act to set light minimum standards in the area of criminal procedures. The Government also believes that qualified majority voting would not be the most appropriate way of proceeding where significant harmonisation of criminal procedural law was concerned.

84. The Government will not give up the UK's right to carry out frontier controls and the Protocols which safeguard the UK's position.

85. The Government supports stronger action to tackle fraud against the Union's financial interests and to strengthen the coordination role of Eurojust in such cases. But we see no need for the creation of a European Public Prosecutor who would have powers to decide – at EU rather than national level – how to investigate and prosecute serious transnational crimes. The Convention has proposed that such a decision could be taken only by unanimity.

Common Foreign and Security Policy

86. The Government welcomes the retention in the Convention's draft Constitutional Treaty of the current Treaty language making clear that the Common Foreign and Security Policy is conducted by the Member States, the European Council, and the Council of Ministers. The Convention also proposes that the roles presently performed by the EU

High Representative, Javier Solana, and the Commissioner for External Affairs, Chris Patten, should be merged into a single job, which might be described as the European Foreign Minister.

87. The Government believes that such a merger would make the European Union more effective in areas where we have a common foreign policy, such as in the Balkans and the Middle East Peace Process. On such issues, our own influence is enhanced by having a common European approach, and a single EU spokesman will both strengthen and streamline this European role. We will of course want to ensure that this representative is properly accountable to Member States in the Council.

88. The Government also welcomes the new linkage between the Common Foreign and Security Policy, including the European Security and Defence Policy, and EU trade policy and development policy, which would all be grouped under one Title of the new Treaty. The Government believes this should improve the overall coherence of EU external action.

Development

89. The EU is an important player in international development. Together, the EU and Member States constitute the world's largest provider of official development assistance. The EU is also the main trading partner of most developing countries.

90. The Government welcomes the draft Treaty's commitment to the eradication of poverty as the primary objective of EU development policy. We believe that the policy should apply to all developing countries. The proposed inclusion of a chapter on humanitarian aid is also useful and would provide clear basis for the EU's efforts in this field.

91. We welcome the draft Treaty's proposal that the EU should take account of development objectives in other policies likely to affect developing countries. We also welcome the clear proposal that the Union and Member States share competence for EU development policy.

92. We will want to ensure that the intergovernmental nature of the European Development Fund, which provides the basis for the Commission's assistance to Africa, the Caribbean and the Pacific, is maintained. This would allow us to meet the needs of those countries most effectively.

ESDP

93. The Government has been a strong supporter of the European Security and Defence Policy (ESDP), which is designed to give the EU the military and civilian capabilities it needs to support the EU's Common Foreign and Security Policy objectives and, in turn, the peace and international security objectives of the UN. We therefore welcome a

number of innovations proposed by the Convention in this area. It is only by strengthening ESDP that we will be able to continue to undertake operations of the kind we have recently seen in Bosnia, Macedonia and the Democratic Republic of Congo.

94. Updating the Petersberg Tasks, which define the range of operations ESDP can undertake,[9] will mean that the stated objectives of ESDP more closely reflect the security challenges we now face. A new 'solidarity' clause should give us a robust mechanism to ensure a swift, coordinated response to a Member State's request for help in dealing with the consequences of a disaster or terrorist attack. And the creation of an intergovernmental Agency to support defence capability development should ensure that improved, more cost-effective, capabilities are made available to ESDP as a result of increased transparency and cooperation among Member States. This is essential to the EU being able to run crisis management operations in an appropriate, timely and effective way.

95. We will not, however, support all the proposals as currently set out in the Convention text. We believe that a flexible, inclusive approach and effective links to NATO are essential to the success of ESDP. We will not agree to anything which is contradictory to, or would replace, the security guarantee established through NATO.

96. Similarly, we already have detailed, and militarily robust, arrangements (which were agreed by all member states at the Nice European Council) to provide for flexibility in ESDP. So any provisions for new forms of cooperation must not undermine these arrangements.

Sustainable development and the environment

97. The Government welcomes the Convention's proposal that, as now, sustainable development should be a primary objective of the Union. The draft makes clear that successful sustainable development requires us to pursue economic, social and environmental objectives at one and the same time. We also support maintaining the provision that environmental protection requirements should be part of all of the Union's activities.

---

[9] The updated Petersberg Tasks proposed in the draft Treaty are: "joint disarmament operations, humanitarian and rescue tasks, military advice and assistance tasks, conflict prevention and peace-keeping tasks, tasks of combat forces in crisis management, including peacemaking, and post-conflict stabilisation. All these tasks may contribute to the fight against terrorism, including by supporting third countries in combating terrorism in their territories." (Article III-210)

The Charter of Fundamental Rights

98. The EU Charter of Fundamental Rights sets down rights, freedoms and principles applicable at EU level. It draws existing fundamental liberties together and makes them more visible to the citizen. The EU should respect these, whenever it acts. The Charter is currently only a political declaration. The IGC will consider whether it should now be incorporated into the draft Constitutional Treaty.

99. Most national Governments already have a list of citizens' basic rights and liberties which the State must respect. The UK has a particularly strong tradition of individual liberties and in 1998 gave further effect to the European Convention on Human Rights (ECHR) in our domestic laws. But the ECHR does not directly control the European Union's institutions. And the ECHR is confined to civil and political rights – it does not cover the voting and other special rights, such as on freedom of movement, to which people are entitled as EU citizens. In any case, there has been no catalogue of rights which applies to the European Union institutions.

100. The UK supports a clear statement of the rights, freedoms and principles EU institutions should respect. We supported the Charter of Rights at Nice nearly three years ago as a political declaration, but it was not clear enough for legal use.

101. We and some other Member States worked hard in the Convention on the Future of Europe to help get more clarity and legal certainty into the Charter. The changes we helped push through have put the whole package in much better legal shape.

102. The Convention text makes clear, in Article II-51, that the Charter "does not extend the field of application of Union law beyond the powers of the Union or establish any new power or task for the Union, or modify powers and tasks defined in the other Parts of the Constitution." It therefore does not give any new powers to the EU. The Member States are affected only when they are implementing Union law. So where Member States are dealing with non-EU matters the Charter has no legal application. The Convention also updated and improved helpful technical Explanations clarifying the legal meaning of the Charter – and agreed that the Courts should have due regard to these.

103. The Government will make a final decision on incorporation of the Charter into the draft Constitutional Treaty only in the light of the overall picture at the IGC.

A History of the Charter of Fundamental Rights

1999   Agreement on need to make rights applicable at EU level more visible – Cologne Council (June).

Agreement on broadly-based Convention to draw up Charter – Tampere Council (October).

2000   Start of drafting process chaired by ex-President of Germany, Roman Herzog (January). Lord Goldsmith QC represents UK.

Charter agreed as a political declaration – Nice Council (December).

2001   Question of Charter's legal status and EU accession to the ECHR agreed for debate – Laeken Council (December).

2002   Convention on the Future of Europe establishes Working Group on Charter – Baroness Scotland QC represents UK.

2003   Convention on the Future of Europe proposes insertion of Charter (as amended) into the draft Constitutional Treaty and revised technical Explanations with legal status.

V.
Conclusion

104. When the IGC starts in October, it will cover issues which touch on many aspects of our lives and the way we govern ourselves. That is the nature of the EU. The Constitutional Treaty that we aim to produce in the IGC will modernise, simplify and clarify the workings of the EU in all of these areas.

105. The Treaty will not, however, change the fundamental relationship between the EU and the Member States. Nor will it change the basic principles of the Union, such as the conferral of competences by the Member States. They will continue to underpin everything the EU does.

106. Instead, the Constitutional Treaty will build on this framework to bring the Union's institutions and policies up to date. It will produce an efficient, transparent and accountable EU, equipped to meet the challenges of the 21st century. That is very much the British agenda.

107. The Government therefore wants the IGC to be a success. It will do its best to ensure that it is. We will take the same positive and constructive approach in the IGC as we took in the Convention and have taken in all of our dealings on Europe. But the Government will not sign up to any treaty which does not, in its view, advance UK interests.

Annex A

Amsterdam Treaty
The Treaty of Amsterdam was agreed in 1997 and entered into force in May 1999. It provided for important changes in the range of matters falling under EC competence – incorporation of the Schengen acquis, moving visas and asylum policy to the first pillar, an employment chapter, and incorporation of the social protocol. Amsterdam also endorsed "the progressive framing of a common defence policy" and extended the use of co-decision and QMV.

Acquis
The phrase *acquis communautaire* refers to the whole range of principles, policies, laws, practices, obligations and objectives that have been agreed within the EU. It includes the Treaties, EU legislation, judgments of the Court of Justice and joint actions taken in the fields of the Common Foreign and Security Policy and Justice and Home Affairs.

Charter of Fundamental Rights
The Charter sets out the fundamental rights applicable at EU level. It was drawn up by a Convention during 2000 and was adopted at the Nice European Council in December 2000. The Convention examined the question of whether, and if so how, the Charter should be given legal status.

College of Commissioners
Formal term for the body of European Commissioners known as the Commission.

Co-decision procedure (article 251 EC)
Introduced by the Treaty of Maastricht, this procedure has been modified by the Treaty of Amsterdam and now applies to most areas of Community legislation. The draft EU Constitutional Treaty would make co-decision the routine legislative procedure. It is a complex process. It involves both the Council and Parliament proposing amendments to a piece of legislation proposed by the Commission. Both need to agree if the draft is to become law. It is a lengthy procedure: it can often take a year or more to approve legislation.

Commission
An EU institution currently made up of 20 Commissioners (two from the UK, France, Germany, Italy, and Spain, one from other Member States). Its President is currently Romano Prodi, former Prime Minister of Italy. The British Commissioners are Chris Patten and Neil Kinnock. It is central to the EU's decision-making process and its successful conduct of business. It has the tasks of ensuring the Treaty is correctly applied, of proposing new legislation to the Council and European Parliament for approval, and of exercising implementing powers given it by the Council.

Common Agricultural Policy (CAP)

The aims of the CAP are: to increase agricultural productivity; to ensure a fair standard of living for the agricultural community; to stabilise markets; to assure the availability of supplies; and to ensure that supplies reach consumers at reasonable prices. To achieve these objectives, the CAP is based on three principles: a single market; Community preference; and financial solidarity. The CAP has been successful in generating food production with the EU, but has been much criticised for its environmental consequences and its effects on developing countries. EU Agriculture Ministers agreed a significant reform of the CAP in June 2003.

Common Foreign and Security Policy (CFSP)

An area of intergovernmental activity within the Union, but outside the European Communities. CFSP covers all areas of foreign and security policy. Its objectives include safeguarding common values; strengthening the security of the Union; preserving international security; promoting international cooperation; and consolidating democracy and the rule of law.

Conclusions

Political agreements reached at the end of European Council meetings. European Council conclusions are produced on the authority of the Presidency only. But they are nevertheless the normal way for the **European Council** to signal a commitment.

COREPER

Coreper stands for the Committee of Permanent Representatives. It is composed of the Member States' ambassadors to the EU and prepares the meetings of the **Council of Ministers**.

Council of Ministers of the European Union

This is the primary decision-making body of the Union. It meets in sectoral formats chaired by the Presidency and attended by the relevant national ministers (e.g. Economic/Finance (ECOFIN) and Competitiveness Councils). They are also attended by the **Commission** (usually the relevant Commissioner). Working Groups and **COREPER** prepare the Council's work. It is supported by the Council Secretariat.

EU High Representative

The representative of the **Council of Ministers** for **Common Foreign and Security Policy** matters. Javier Solana was appointed High Representative for the CFSP in June 1999 by the Cologne **European Council**. He is also Secretary-General of the Council and, as such, head of the Council Secretariat.

Euratom

Also known at the European Atomic Energy Community (E.A.E.C.), Euratom was established in 1957, at the same time as the European Economic Community. Its responsibilities include research and information, health and safety, investment and safeguards as they relate to the atomic energy industry. The Euratom Supply Agency is responsible for supply.

Eurojust

Formally known as the European Judicial Cooperation Unit, Eurojust was created by the Tampere European Council in October 1999. It is a body of national prosecutors, magistrates and police officers from each **Member State** which works to ensure cooperation between national authorities and to support investigations into organised crime.

European Community

See **European Union**.

European Council

A summit of Heads of State or Government that has met regularly since the 1970s. It now normally meets four times a year, twice under each six-monthly Presidency. Originally an informal gathering, the European Council was given formal recognition in the **Single European Act** of 1986. It has the task of providing the EU with the necessary impetus for its development and defining the necessary general political guidelines for its work. These meetings are sometimes referred to as European Summits. The European Council will normally agree **Conclusions**.

European Court of Justice (ECJ)

The European Court of Justice is made up of Judges appointed by the **Member States**. It has the task of ensuring that the law is observed in the interpretation and application of the Treaty. It therefore rules on questions relating to interpretation of the Treaties, and secondary legislation in direct actions and in cases referred to it by national courts. ECJ judgments form part of national law. It also has certain powers in relation to certain **Third Pillar** measures, but no jurisdiction over **CFSP**. There is also a Court of First Instance to deal with certain specified issues.

European Parliament (EP)

The European Parliament is composed of 626 members (87 from the UK), directly elected every five years in each Member State. These numbers will change to reflect enlargement in 2004. Originally a consultative body, successive Treaties have increased the EP's role in scrutinising the activities of the **Commission** and extended its legislative and budgetary powers. The Parliament meets in plenary session in Strasbourg and Brussels. The next EP elections will be in June 2004.

European Union

The European Union was created by the Treaty of Maastricht in 1992 (also called the Treaty on European Union or TEU). It currently consists of three pillars. The First Pillar is the pre-existing European Community, which covers largely, though by no means exclusively, economic business. The EU institutions are fully involved in the decision-making process. The Second Pillar is the **Common Foreign and Security Policy**. The Third Pillar, after amendment by the Treaty of Amsterdam, covers certain police and judicial cooperation in criminal matters. The main difference between the **First Pillar** and the rest is that under the latter Member States, as well as the Commission, have the right to propose policies, and that the **European Court of Justice** does not have jurisdiction, with the exception of parts of the Third Pillar under certain circumstances. The new Constitutional Treaty will dissolve the three pillars to create a single Treaty structure.

Europol

At the Luxembourg **European Council** in December 1991, **Member States** decided to create an organisation to facilitate police cooperation in the EU. The Europol Convention came into force in October 1998. Europol currentlysupports operations which Member States initiate and investigate, in order to fight serious cross-border crime such as drug smuggling, people trafficking, car theft and money laundering.

European Security and Defence Policy

The European Security and Defence Policy is a British initiative launched by the Prime Minister, together with the French Government, in 1998. It centres on strengthening Europe's capability for crisis management through both NATO and the EU. The policy is designed to give the EU the tools to take on humanitarian and peace-keeping tasks when NATO is not engaged.

First pillar

See **European Union**.

Implementation

The application and enforcement of Community law within the **Member States**, once it has been transposed into national law where necessary.

Legal base (or basis)

The article of the EU Treaties that gives the Union the right to act is often called the legal base. It also describes the voting procedure and type of legislative procedure (e.g. co-decision) that should be used.

Lisbon economic reform agenda or Lisbon process

In Lisbon in March 2000 the **European Council** set itself a new strategic goal for the next decade: "to become the most competitive and dynamic knowledge-based economy in the world, capable of sustainable economic growth with more and better jobs and greater social cohesion." Progress towards this goal is reviewed at successive spring **European Councils**.

Maastricht Treaty
See European Union.

Member State
A country which is a member of the European Union.

Nice Treaty
The Treaty of Nice was agreed at the Nice European Council in December 2000 and came into force in 2003. It set out new arrangements for the size and composition of the European Commission, and agreed reforms to the system of Qualified Majority Voting in Council while extending it to a number of new policy areas. The box on page 22 gives more details.

Praesidium
The Praesidium was a steering group for the Convention on the Future of Europe. It was led by Valéry Giscard d'Estaing and had twelve other members representing a cross-section of the Convention's membership, including government delegates and representatives from the Accession states. Gisela Stuart MP and John Bruton from Ireland represented national parliamentarians.

Presidency
This is in effect the chairmanship of the European Union. The Presidency rotates every six months among the Member States. Italy will hold the Presidency from July to December 2003, Ireland from January to June 2004. The next UK Presidency will be in the second half of 2005. The Presidency chairs most Working Groups, COREPER and meetings of the Council of Ministers and is important in setting the Union's agenda and working towards an agreement. The Convention has proposed some changes to the Presidency arrangements.

Qualified majority voting (QMV)
This is a voting mechanism in the Council under which a proposal can be adopted without every Member State agreeing to it. Under the current arrangements, for a proposal to be adopted it needs 62 votes from Member States in favour, out of the total of 87 weighted votes. The UK has 10 such votes. These weights will change following enlargement.

Schengen acquis
"Schengen" is the shorthand for measures originally agreed in 1985, in the Luxembourg village of Schengen, by certain Member States on the gradual elimination of border controls at their common frontiers. These agreements were incorporated into the Treaties with the Treaty of Amsterdam in 1999. The UK and Ireland have applied to participate in the police and judicial cooperation elements of the Schengen acquis but have not sought to participate in the external border measures. The UK and Ireland are only bound by the Schengen acquis if they choose to opt-in to its provisions, and have the specific right, set out in the Treaty, to maintain their border controls.

Second pillar
Deals with **Common Foreign and Security Policy**.

Single European Act
This Treaty, which was agreed in 1986 and entered into force iin 1987, was the first substantial revision of the Community Treaties. Among the main changes it made were the initiation of cooperation in environment policy and foreign policy; the extension of **qualified majority voting** (notably to allow the rapid development of the **Single Market**); the granting of a greater role in legislation to the **European Parliament**; and the setting up of the **Court of First Instance**. It also gave the first formal Treaty recognition to the **European Council**.

Single Market
Shorthand for the EU's commitment to create an internal market in which all obstacles to the free movement of goods, persons, services and capital between Member States have been abolished. The Single Market was largely completed by 1992 but remains incomplete in some areas. A major aim of the **Lisbon Process** is to accelerate its full completion and implementation.

Subsidiarity
The concept that action should only be taken by the Community only if and in so far as the objectives of the proposed action cannot be sufficiently achieved by the **Member States** and can therefore be better achieved at European level. This concept is enshrined in the Treaty.

Third Pillar
See **European Union**.

Unanimity
A form of voting in the Council. A proposal requiring unanimity must have no **Member State** voting against (abstentions do not matter). See also **Qualified majority voting**.

For further information

www.european-convention.int.eu
http://europa.eu.int/futurum/index_en.htm

**NICE EUROPEAN COUNCIL MEETING
7, 8 AND 9 DECEMBER 2000**

DECLARATION ON THE FUTURE OF EUROPE

1. Important reforms have been decided in Nice. The Conference welcomes the successful conclusion of the Conference of Representatives of the Governments of the Member States and commits the Member States to pursue the early ratification of the Treaty of Nice.

2. It agrees that the conclusion of the Conference of Representatives of the Governments of the Member States opens the way for enlargement of the European Union and underlines that, with ratification of the Treaty of Nice, the European Union will have completed the institutional changes necessary for the accession of new Member States.

3. Having thus opened the way to enlargement, the Conference calls for a deeper and wider debate about the future of the European Union. In 2001, the Swedish and Belgian Presidencies, in cooperation with the Commission and involving the European Parliament, will encourage wide-ranging discussions with all interested parties: representatives of national parliaments and all those reflecting public opinion, namely political, economic and university circles, representatives of civil society, etc. The candidate States will be associated with this process in ways to be defined.

4. Following a report to be drawn up for the European Council in Göteborg in June 2001, the European Council, at its meeting in Laeken/Brussels in December 2001, will agree on a declaration containing appropriate initiatives for the continuation of this process.

5. The process should address, *inter alia*, the following questions:

   – how to establish and monitor a more precise delimitation of powers between the European Union and the Member States, reflecting the principle of subsidiarity;

   – the status of the Charter of Fundamental Rights of the European Union proclaimed in Nice, in accordance with the conclusions of the European Council in Cologne;

   – a simplification of the Treaties with a view to making them clearer and better understood without changing their meaning;

   – the role of national parliaments in the European architecture.

6. Addressing the abovementioned issues, the Conference recognises the need to improve and to monitor the democratic legitimacy and transparency of the Union and its institutions, in order to bring them closer to the citizens of the Member States.

7. After these preparatory steps, the Conference agrees that a new Conference of the Representatives of the Governments of the Member States will be convened in 2004, to address the abovementioned items with a view to making corresponding changes to the Treaties.

8. The Conference of Member States shall not constitute any form of obstacle or pre-condition to the enlargement process. Moreover, those candidate States which have concluded accession negotiations with the Union will be invited to participate in the Conference. Those candidate States which have not concluded their accession negotiations will be invited as observers.

EUROPEAN COUNCIL MEETING IN LAEKEN

14 AND 15 DECEMBER 2001

**ANNEX I TO
PRESIDENCY CONCLUSIONS**

**LAEKEN DECLARATION
ON THE FUTURE OF THE EUROPEAN UNION**

I. EUROPE AT A CROSSROADS

For centuries, peoples and states have taken up arms and waged war to win control of the European continent. The debilitating effects of two bloody wars and the weakening of Europe's position in the world brought a growing realisation that only peace and concerted action could make the dream of a strong, unified Europe come true. In order to banish once and for all the demons of the past, a start was made with a coal and steel community. Other economic activities, such as agriculture, were subsequently added in. A genuine single market was eventually established for goods, persons, services and capital, and a single currency was added in 1999. On 1 January 2002 the euro is to become a day-to-day reality for 300 million European citizens.

The European Union has thus gradually come into being. In the beginning, it was more of an economic and technical collaboration. Twenty years ago, with the first direct elections to the European Parliament, the Community's democratic legitimacy, which until then had lain with the Council alone, was considerably strengthened. Over the last ten years, construction of a political union has begun and cooperation been established on social policy, employment, asylum, immigration, police, justice, foreign policy and a common security and defence policy.

The European Union is a success story. For over half a century now, Europe has been at peace. Along with North America and Japan, the Union forms one of the three most prosperous parts of the world. As a result of mutual solidarity and fair distribution of the benefits of economic development, moreover, the standard of living in the Union's weaker regions has increased enormously and they have made good much of the disadvantage they were at.

Fifty years on, however, the Union stands at a crossroads, a defining moment in its existence. The unification of Europe is near. The Union is about to expand to bring in more than ten new Member States, predominantly Central and Eastern European, thereby finally closing one of the darkest chapters in European history: the Second World War and the ensuing artificial division of Europe. At long last, Europe is on its way to becoming one big family, without bloodshed, a real transformation clearly calling for a different approach from fifty years ago, when six countries first took the lead.

The democratic challenge facing Europe

At the same time, the Union faces twin challenges, one within and the other beyond its borders.

Within the Union, the European institutions must be brought closer to its citizens. Citizens undoubtedly support the Union's broad aims, but they do not always see a connection between those goals and the Union's everyday action. They want the European institutions to be less unwieldy and rigid and, above all, more efficient and open. Many also feel that the Union should involve itself more with their particular concerns, instead of intervening, in every detail, in matters by their nature better left to Member States' and regions' elected representatives. This is even perceived by some as a threat to their identity. More importantly, however, they feel that deals are all too often cut out of their sight and they want better democratic scrutiny.

Europe's new role in a globalised world

Beyond its borders, in turn, the European Union is confronted with a fast-changing, globalised world. Following the fall of the Berlin Wall, it looked briefly as though we would for a long while be living in a stable world order, free from conflict, founded upon human rights. Just a few years later, however, there is no such certainty. The eleventh of September has brought a rude awakening. The opposing forces have not gone away: religious fanaticism, ethnic nationalism, racism and terrorism are on the increase, and regional conflicts, poverty and underdevelopment still provide a constant seedbed for them.

What is Europe's role in this changed world? Does Europe not, now that is finally unified, have a leading role to play in a new world order, that of a power able both to play a stabilising role worldwide and to point the way ahead for many countries and peoples? Europe as the continent of humane values, the Magna Carta, the Bill of Rights, the French Revolution and the fall of the Berlin Wall; the continent of liberty, solidarity and above all diversity, meaning respect for others' languages, cultures and traditions. The European Union's one boundary is democracy and human rights. The Union is open only to countries which uphold basic values such as free elections, respect for minorities and respect for the rule of law.

Now that the Cold War is over and we are living in a globalised, yet also highly fragmented world, Europe needs to shoulder its responsibilities in the governance of globalisation. The role it has to play is that of a power resolutely doing battle against all violence, all terror and all fanaticism, but which also does not turn a blind eye to the world's heartrending injustices. In short, a power wanting to change the course of world affairs in such a way as to benefit not just the rich countries but also the poorest. A power seeking to set globalisation within a moral framework, in other words to anchor it in solidarity and sustainable development.

The expectations of Europe's citizens

The image of a democratic and globally engaged Europe admirably matches citizens' wishes. There have been frequent public calls for a greater EU role in justice and security, action against cross-border crime, control of migration flows and reception of asylum seekers and refugees from far-flung war zones. Citizens also want results in the fields of employment and combating poverty and social exclusion, as well as in the field of economic and social cohesion. They want a common approach on environmental pollution, climate change and food safety, in short, all transnational issues which they instinctively sense can only be tackled by working together. Just as they also want to see Europe more involved in foreign affairs, security and defence, in other words, greater and better coordinated action to deal with trouble spots in and around Europe and in the rest of the world.

At the same time, citizens also feel that the Union is behaving too bureaucratically in numerous other areas. In coordinating the economic, financial and fiscal environment, the basic issue should continue to be proper operation of the internal market and the single currency, without this jeopardising Member States' individuality. National and regional differences frequently stem from history or tradition. They can be enriching. In other words, what citizens understand by "good governance" is opening up fresh opportunities, not imposing further red tape. What they expect is more results, better responses to practical issues and not a European superstate or European institutions inveigling their way into every nook and cranny of life.

In short, citizens are calling for a clear, open, effective, democratically controlled Community approach, developing a Europe which points the way ahead for the world. An approach that provides concrete results in terms of more jobs, better quality of life, less crime, decent education and better health care. There can be no doubt that this will require Europe to undergo renewal and reform.

II. CHALLENGES AND REFORMS IN A RENEWED UNION

The Union needs to become more democratic, more transparent and more efficient. It also has to resolve three basic challenges: how to bring citizens, and primarily the young, closer to the European design and the European institutions, how to organise politics and the European political area in an enlarged Union and how to develop the Union into a stabilising factor and a model in the new, multipolar world. In order to address them a number of specific questions need to be put.

A better division and definition of competence in the European Union

Citizens often hold expectations of the European Union that are not always fulfilled. And vice versa – they sometimes have the impression that the Union takes on too much in areas where its involvement is not always essential. Thus the important thing is to clarify, simplify and adjust the division of competence between the Union and the Member States in the light of the new challenges facing the Union. This can lead both to restoring tasks to the Member States and to assigning new missions to the Union, or to the extension of existing powers, while constantly bearing in mind the equality of the Member States and their mutual solidarity.

A first series of questions that needs to be put concerns how the division of competence can be made more transparent. Can we thus make a clearer distinction between three types of competence: the exclusive competence of the Union, the competence of the Member States and the shared competence of the Union and the Member States? At what level is competence exercised in the most efficient way? How is the principle of subsidiarity to be applied here? And should we not make it clear that any powers not assigned by the Treaties to the Union fall within the exclusive sphere of competence of the Member States? And what would be the consequences of this?

The next series of questions should aim, within this new framework and while respecting the "acquis communautaire", to determine whether there needs to be any reorganisation of competence. How can citizens' expectations be taken as a guide here? What missions would this produce for the Union? And, vice versa, what tasks could better be left to the Member States? What amendments should be made to the Treaty on the various policies? How, for example, should a more coherent common foreign policy and defence policy be developed? Should the Petersberg tasks be updated? Do we want to adopt a more integrated approach to police and criminal law cooperation? How can economic-policy coordination be stepped up? How can we intensify cooperation in the field of social inclusion, the environment, health and food safety? But then, should not the day-to-day administration and implementation of the Union's policy be left more emphatically to the Member States and, where their constitutions so provide, to the regions? Should they not be provided with guarantees that their spheres of competence will not be affected?

Lastly, there is the question of how to ensure that a redefined division of competence does not lead to a creeping expansion of the competence of the Union or to encroachment upon the exclusive areas of competence of the Member States and, where there is provision for this, regions. How are we to ensure at the same time that the European dynamic does not come to a halt? In the future as well the Union must continue to be able to react to fresh challenges and developments and must be able to explore new policy areas. Should Articles 95 and 308 of the Treaty be reviewed for this purpose in the light of the "acquis jurisprudentiel"?

Simplification of the Union's instruments

Who does what is not the only important question; the nature of the Union's action and what instruments it should use are equally important. Successive amendments to the Treaty have on each occasion resulted in a proliferation of instruments, and directives have gradually evolved towards more and more detailed legislation. The key question is therefore whether the Union's various instruments should not be better defined and whether their number should not be reduced.

In other words, should a distinction be introduced between legislative and executive measures? Should the number of legislative instruments be reduced: directly applicable rules, framework legislation and non-enforceable instruments (opinions, recommendations, open coordination)? Is it or is it not desirable to have more frequent recourse to framework legislation, which affords the Member States more room for manoeuvre in achieving policy objectives? For which areas of competence are open coordination and mutual recognition the most appropriate instruments? Is the principle of proportionality to remain the point of departure?

More democracy, transparency and efficiency in the European Union

The European Union derives its legitimacy from the democratic values it projects, the aims it pursues and the powers and instruments it possesses. However, the European project also derives its legitimacy from democratic, transparent and efficient institutions. The national parliaments also contribute towards the legitimacy of the European project. The declaration on the future of the Union, annexed to the Treaty of Nice, stressed the need to examine their role in European integration. More generally, the question arises as to what initiatives we can take to develop a European public area.

The first question is thus how we can increase the democratic legitimacy and transparency of the present institutions, a question which is valid for the three institutions.

How can the authority and efficiency of the European Commission be enhanced? How should the President of the Commission be appointed: by the European Council, by the European Parliament or should he be directly elected by the citizens? Should the role of the European Parliament be strengthened? Should we extend the right of co-decision or not? Should the way in which we elect the members of the European Parliament be reviewed? Should a European electoral constituency be created, or should constituencies continue to be determined nationally? Can the two systems be combined? Should the role of the Council be strengthened? Should the Council act in the same manner in its legislative and its executive capacities? With a view to greater transparency, should the meetings of the Council, at least in its legislative capacity, be public? Should citizens have more access to Council documents? How, finally, should the balance and reciprocal control between the institutions be ensured?

A second question, which also relates to democratic legitimacy, involves the role of national parliaments. Should they be represented in a new institution, alongside the Council and the European Parliament? Should they have a role in areas of European action in which the European Parliament has no competence? Should they focus on the division of competence between Union and Member States, for example through preliminary checking of compliance with the principle of subsidiarity?

The third question concerns how we can improve the efficiency of decision-making and the workings of the institutions in a Union of some thirty Member States. How could the Union set its objectives and priorities more effectively and ensure better implementation? Is there a need for more decisions by a qualified majority? How is the co-decision procedure between the Council and the European Parliament to be simplified and speeded up? What of the six-monthly rotation of the Presidency of the Union? What is the future role of the European Parliament? What of the future role and structure of the various Council formations? How should the coherence of European foreign policy be enhanced? How is synergy between the High Representative and the competent Commissioner to be reinforced? Should the external representation of the Union in international fora be extended further?

Towards a Constitution for European citizens

The European Union currently has four Treaties. The objectives, powers and policy instruments of the Union are currently spread across those Treaties. If we are to have greater transparency, simplification is essential.

Four sets of questions arise in this connection. The first concerns simplifying the existing Treaties without changing their content. Should the distinction between the Union and the Communities be reviewed? What of the division into three pillars?

Questions then arise as to the possible reorganisation of the Treaties. Should a distinction be made between a basic treaty and the other treaty provisions? Should this distinction involve separating the texts? Could this lead to a distinction between the amendment and ratification procedures for the basic treaty and for the other treaty provisions?

Thought would also have to be given to whether the Charter of Fundamental Rights should be included in the basic treaty and to whether the European Community should accede to the European Convention on Human Rights.

The question ultimately arises as to whether this simplification and reorganisation might not lead in the long run to the adoption of a constitutional text in the Union. What might the basic features of such a constitution be? The values which the Union cherishes, the fundamental rights and obligations of its citizens, the relationship between Member States in the Union?

iii. CONVENING OF A CONVENTION ON THE FUTURE OF EUROPE

In order to pave the way for the next Intergovernmental Conference as broadly and openly as possible, the European Council has decided to convene a Convention composed of the main parties involved in the debate on the future of the Union. In the light of the foregoing, it will be the task of that Convention to consider the key issues arising for the Union's future development and try to identify the various possible responses.

The European Council has appointed Mr V. Giscard d'Estaing as Chairman of the Convention and Mr G. Amato and Mr J.L. Dehaene as Vice-Chairmen.

Composition

In addition to its Chairman and Vice-Chairmen, the Convention will be composed of 15 representatives of the Heads of State or Government of the Member States (one from each Member State), 30 members of national parliaments (two from each Member State), 16 members of the European Parliament and two Commission representatives. The accession candidate countries will be fully involved in the Convention's proceedings. They will be represented in the same way as the current Member States (one government representative and two national parliament members) and will be able to take part in the proceedings without, however, being able to prevent any consensus which may emerge among the Member States.

The members of the Convention may only be replaced by alternate members if they are not present. The alternate members will be designated in the same way as full members.

The Praesidium of the Convention will be composed of the Convention Chairman and Vice-Chairmen and nine members drawn from the Convention (the representatives of all the governments holding the Council Presidency during the Convention, two national parliament representatives, two European Parliament representatives and two Commission representatives).

Three representatives of the Economic and Social Committee with three representatives of the European social partners; from the Committee of the Regions: six representatives (to be appointed by the Committee of the Regions from the regions, cities and regions with legislative powers), and the European Ombudsman will be invited to attend as observers. The Presidents of the Court of Justice and of the Court of Auditors may be invited by the Praesidium to address the Convention.

Length of proceedings

The Convention will hold its inaugural meeting on 1 March 2002, when it will appoint its Praesidium and adopt its rules of procedure. Proceedings will be completed after a year, that is to say in time for the Chairman of the Convention to present its outcome to the European Council.

Working methods

The Chairman will pave the way for the opening of the Convention's proceedings by drawing conclusions from the public debate. The Praesidium will serve to lend impetus and will provide the Convention with an initial working basis.

The Praesidium may consult Commission officials and experts of its choice on any technical aspect which it sees fit to look into. It may set up ad hoc working parties.

The Council will be kept informed of the progress of the Convention's proceedings. The Convention Chairman will give an oral progress report at each European Council meeting, thus enabling Heads of State or Government to give their views at the same time.

The Convention will meet in Brussels. The Convention's discussions and all official documents will be in the public domain. The Convention will work in the Union's eleven working languages.

Final document

The Convention will consider the various issues. It will draw up a final document which may comprise either different options, indicating the degree of support which they received, or recommendations if consensus is achieved.

Together with the outcome of national debates on the future of the Union, the final document will provide a starting point for discussions in the Intergovernmental Conference, which will take the ultimate decisions.

Forum

In order for the debate to be broadly based and involve all citizens, a Forum will be opened for organisations representing civil society (the social partners, the business world, non-governmental organisations, academia, etc.). It will take the form of a structured network of organisations receiving regular information on the Convention's proceedings. Their contributions will serve as input into the debate. Such organisations may be heard or consulted on specific topics in accordance with arrangements to be established by the Praesidium.

Secretariat

The Praesidium will be assisted by a Convention Secretariat, to be provided by the General Secretariat of the Council, which may incorporate Commission and European Parliament experts.

**THESSALONIKI EUROPEAN COUNCIL
19 AND 20 JUNE 2003**

PRESIDENCY CONCLUSIONS

1. The European Council met in Thessaloniki on 19 and 20 June 2003. The meeting was preceded by an exposé by the President of the European Parliament, Mr Pat Cox, followed by an exchange of views concerning the main items on the agenda.

CONVENTION / IGC

2. The European Council welcomes the Draft Constitutional Treaty presented by the President of the Convention, Valéry Giscard d'Estaing. This presentation marks a historic step in the direction of furthering the objectives of European integration:

    – bringing our Union closer to its citizens,

    – strengthening our Union's democratic character,

    – facilitating our Union's capacity to make decisions, especially after its enlargement,

    – enhancing our Union's ability to act as a coherent and unified force in the international system, and

    – effectively deal with the challenges globalisation and interdependence create.

3. The European Council expresses its gratitude to the President of the Convention, Valéry Giscard d'Estaing, the Vice-Presidents, Jean Luc Dehaene and Giuliano Amato, the members and the alternate members of the Convention for the work they have accomplished. The Convention has proven its usefulness as a forum for democratic dialogue between representatives of governments, national parliaments, the European Parliament, the European Commission and civic society.

4. The European Council considers that the presentation of the Draft Constitutional Treaty, as it has received it, marks the completion of the Convention's tasks as set out at Laeken and, accordingly, the end of its work. However, some purely technical work on drafting Part III is still required, this work needing to be finished by 15 July at the latest.

5. The European Council decided that the text of the Draft Constitutional Treaty is a good basis for starting in the Intergovernmental Conference. It requests the future Italian Presidency to initiate, at the Council meeting in July, the procedure laid down in Article 48 of the Treaty in order to allow this Conference to be convened in October 2003. The Conference

should complete its work and agree the Constitutional Treaty as soon as possible and in time for it to become known to European citizens before the June 2004 elections for the European Parliament. The acceding States will participate fully in the Intergovernmental Conference on an equal footing with the current Member States. The Constitutional Treaty will be signed by the Member States of the enlarged Union as soon as possible after 1 May 2004.

6. The Intergovernmental Conference will be conducted by the Heads of State or Government, assisted by the members of the General Affairs and External Relations Council. The representative of the Commission will participate in the Conference. The General Secretariat of the Council will provide the secretariat support for the Conference. The European Parliament will be closely associated and involved in the work of the Conference.

7. The three candidate countries – Bulgaria and Romania, with whom accession negotiations are underway, and Turkey – will take part in all meetings of the Conference as observers.

Printed in the UK by the Stationery Office Limited
on behalf of the Controller of Her Majesty's Stationery Office
08/03   019585   ID154609